A Taste
of culture

Foods of China

Barbara Sheen

3 1389 01831 4302

KIDHAVEN PRESS

An imprint of Thomson Gale, a part of The Thomson Corporation

THOMSON

™

GALE

Detroit • New York • San Francisco • San Diego • New Haven, Conn. • Waterville, Maine • London • Munich

© 2006 by KidHaven Press. KidHaven Press is an imprint of The Gale Group, Inc., a division of Thomson Learning, Inc.

KidHaven™ and Thomson Learning™ are trademarks used herein under license.

For more information, contact
KidHaven Press
27500 Drake Rd.
Farmington Hills, MI 48331-3535
Or you can visit our Internet site at http://www.gale.com

LIBRARY OF CONGRESS CATALOGING-IN-PUBLICATION DATA
Sheen, Barbara.
Foods of China / by Barbara Sheen.
p. cm. — (A taste of culture)
Includes bibliographical references and index.
ISBN 0-7377-3031-5 (hard cover: alk. paper)
1. Cookery, Chinese—Juvenile literature. 2. China—Social life and customs—Juvenile literature. I. Title. II. Series.
TX724.5.C5S534 2005
394.1'2'0951—dc22
2005015765

Printed in the United States of America

Contents

4/07

Chapter 1

A Common Thread

Chinese food is one of the most delicious cuisines on Earth. It is also one of the most varied cuisines. As the third largest nation in the world, China has a wide range of geographic regions. Different foods are found in China's many regions. In the north, fields of wheat paint the landscape gold and provide flour for noodles. The many waterways in southern and eastern China make fish and seafood abundant. In the west, hot peppers and citrus fruits add zest to local dishes. Despite these regional variations, three foods—rice, vegetables, and soybeans—form a common thread that is woven through all Chinese cooking.

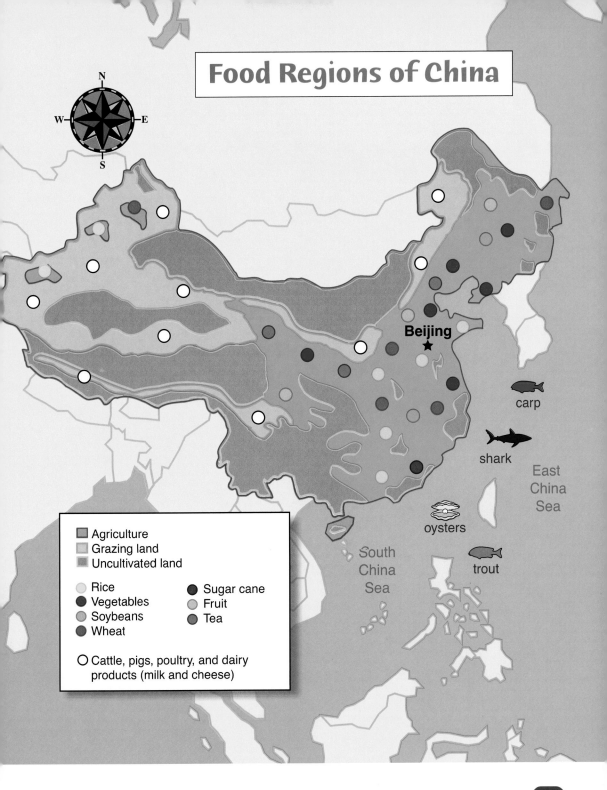

Food Regions of China

N
W E
S

Beijing ★

carp

shark

oysters

East China Sea

South China Sea

trout

Agriculture
Grazing land
Uncultivated land

○ Rice
● Vegetables
○ Soybeans
● Wheat

● Sugar cane
○ Fruit
● Tea

○ Cattle, pigs, poultry, and dairy products (milk and cheese)

Chinese farmers grow rice in terraced paddies like this one to provide food for China's 1.3 billion people.

A Basic Necessity

People in China say that the basic necessities for life are rice, clothing, and shelter. That is because *fan*, the Chinese word for "rice," also means "food."

For thousands of years, Chinese fields have produced at least two rice crops a year. This is important because, despite China's size, only 13 percent of its land is suitable for growing food. As a result, food shortages have been common throughout China's history. No matter how scarce other foods were, however, there was always rice.

Even today, when food is plentiful, every Chinese family keeps a large container with as much as 100 pounds (45kg) of uncooked rice in the kitchen. Chinese chef Eileen Yin-Fei Lo recalls, "This demonstrated to us, as well as to others who might see it, that our family was . . . provided for."[1]

From Morning to Night

The average Chinese person eats four bowls of rice a day. Not just any rice will do, however. The Chinese prefer unseasoned, long grain white rice. This rice must be washed thoroughly, then boiled or **steamed** until it is dry and fluffy.

The Chinese use rice as the basis for a variety of dishes, including congee *(con-gee)*, a thin porridge topped with fish or an egg. They blend rice with spinach to make green rice. They burn it and pour hot broth over it to make a sizzling dish called guo bah *(gar-bah)*. They make flour, vinegar, and wine from it. Because rice is so precious, not a grain is wasted. Fried rice is a delicious dish made from leftover rice that is fried with bits of meat, vegetables, and egg.

At a typical Chinese meal, a large bowl of rice is set in the center of the table. Smaller bowls of chicken, meat, seafood, and vegetables surround the rice. Although these foods add flavor, rice is the foundation of the meal.

Chinese Rice

Rice is an essential part of Chinese cooking. The Chinese carefully rinse their rice before cooking it. This cleans the rice and keeps it from becoming sticky. Long grain rice is preferred.

Ingredients:
2 cups long grain white rice
3 cups water

Instructions:
1. Pour the rice into a colander or strainer. Put the strainer in the sink. Run cold water over the rice and stir the rice until the water runs clear.
2. Drain the rice.
3. Put the rice in a three-quart saucepan and add the water. Bring the water to a boil.
4. Reduce the heat to low and cover the saucepan. Let the rice cook for about twenty minutes, until the liquid is absorbed.
5. Fluff the rice with a fork.

Serves 4

A popular restaurant serves its customers a variety of delectable dishes.

The Chinese love rice's pure flavor. They eat it morning, noon, and night. In fact their words for *lunch* and *supper* mean "afternoon rice" and "evening rice." When guests are invited to dine, they are asked to "come and eat rice." Chinese American chef, Grace Young, whose family lived for years in China, explains: "My family ate rice every day and never got tired of it."[2]

Strange and Delicious Vegetables

Nothing goes better with rice than vegetables. That may be why the Chinese eat at least five servings a day.

A Chinese Meal

A typical Chinese meal is different from a meal in North America. Each place setting includes a pair of chopsticks, a porcelain spoon, two bowls—one for rice and the other for soup—and a small plate for meat and vegetables. Knives are not placed on the table. They are used only in cooking.

The food is served in no particular order. Bowls of rice, meat, and vegetables are placed in the center of the table, and the diners help themselves to whatever they want. Soup, however, is often eaten last. The Chinese say this is good for the digestion.

For them, rice accompanied by a mix of vegetables is a delicious meal. Vegetables also add taste and bright color to meat and fish dishes, which are never served without them.

The choice of vegetables is mind-boggling. More than 150 different varieties of vegetables grow in China. Among everyone's favorites are snow peas. These flat, edible pea pods taste almost as sweet as candy. Crunchy, silvery bean sprouts are another top choice. Bok choy, a Chinese cabbage with a peppery flavor, is another. Baby corn, which is no bigger than an adult's fingertip, is so sweet and tender that even the cob is edible. Water chestnuts and lotus and taro roots are nutty-flavored tubers similar to potatoes that grow in Chinese waterways. Crunchy bamboo shoots are cut from bamboo plants as soon as they start to sprout. The delicious selection of vegetables is almost endless.

Fresh and Young

It is a good thing that the Chinese have so many choices, because they insist on eating only the freshest and youngest vegetables. These vegetables have a sweet, clean taste, while older vegetables taste bitter. This is why many cooks shop for vegetables two or three times a day. Yin-Fei Lo recalls that her grandmother "would eat no vegetables that were older than two hours out of the ground, which necessitated repeated trips to the markets."[3]

Once the best vegetables are selected, they are carefully prepared. The Chinese never boil their vegetables.

Shoppers find a wide variety of fresh produce in an open-air market.

Instead they steam or **stir-fry** them. Both methods cook the vegetables rapidly. Rapid cooking leaves the vegetables crisp, hot, and brightly colored. The results are simply delectable.

"Meat Without the Bones"

Perhaps the most popular vegetable in China is the soybean. It has been a part of Chinese cooking since 3000 B.C. The Chinese rarely eat the bean by itself. Instead

Delicious Broccoli

This method of cooking broccoli is simple and scrumptious. Other vegetables such as bok choy, long beans, or snow peas can be prepared in the same way. So can a mix of different vegetables.

Ingredients:

1 pound broccoli
2 tablespoons vegetable oil
1 tablespoon soy sauce
1 teaspoon sugar
1 tablespoon rice vinegar

Instructions:

1. Wash the broccoli in a colander and drain it. Cut off the hard bottoms of the stalks and then cut them lengthwise so that each is no larger than half inch in diameter.
2. Combine the soy sauce, sugar, and vinegar in a small bowl. Mix well.
3. Heat a frying pan or wok over high heat for 45 seconds. Add the oil and heat it until it is very hot, about 325°F.
4. Put the broccoli in the pan. Stir-fry (stir continuously as the food cooks) for two minutes.
5. Pour the soy sauce mixture over the broccoli. Stir-fry for 45 seconds.
6. Serve with rice.

Serves 4

Street vendors offer passersby tofu barbecued on a stick.

they use it to make a number of different sauces. They also turn it into bean curd or **tofu**.

Tofu is a creamy block of soybean curd. Because tofu is loaded with protein, the Chinese often eat it instead of meat. In fact the Chinese call tofu "meat without the bones." It comes in a variety of textures, all of which have a bland taste that takes on the flavor of the foods it is cooked with.

The Chinese use tofu in everything from soups to sweets. They eat it fresh, cooked, chilled, pressed, and **fermented**. They are very picky about what type of tofu goes best in a particular dish. For instance, because it is creamy like pudding, soft tofu is topped with a sugary syrup to make soft silken tofu. This is a popular dessert. Firm tofu is finely diced and fried with vegetables and soy sauce. Some Chinese cooks even carve pressed tofu, which is dried until it becomes as hard as a block of cheese, to look like chicken or fish. Fermented tofu is added to spicy stews or barbecued and served on a stick. Its nickname, "stinky tofu," comes from its strong scent. Sold in jars all over China, it is as soft as custard. Depending on the ingredients it is fermented in, it can be snow white or bright red.

Essential Sauces

The Chinese also use fermented soybeans to make special sauces. These are used as marinades, spices, or dipping sauces. Depending on the ingredients added to the mixture, soybean sauces may be spicy sweet, like reddish brown hoisin sauce, or rich and smoky, like dark brown oyster sauce. Hoisin sauce is made with garlic and sugar, while oyster sauce is made with oyster extract. **Soy sauce**, which is probably the most well-known Chinese sauce, is dark and salty. It is one of the classic flavors of Chinese food. In fact, a favorite Chinese meal involves dipping **dumplings** into soy sauce. No Chinese household is without this special sauce.

Every Chinese cook's kitchen has rice, vegetables, tofu, and soybean sauces on hand. They are essential parts of Chinese food and common threads that tie the Chinese people together.

Soybean

Chapter 2

A Harmony of Flavors

The Chinese have created an incredible array of delicious dishes. Every region has its unique specialties. There are noodle dishes in the north, stir-fries in the south, spicy dishes in the west, and sweet-and-sour dishes in the east.

Although recipes may differ, these favorites have one thing in common: Their ingredients are carefully balanced so that each brings out the best qualities of the others. Making sure that foods complement each other is so important in Chinese cooking that an ancient Chinese proverb advises: "If one hopes to become a good cook, he must first become a good matchmaker; the flavors and ingredients must be 'married' and harmonized."[4]

China's favorite dishes demonstrate this harmony of flavors. It is not surprising that they are beloved by people throughout China. Their scrumptious tastes have no boundaries.

Noodles

The Chinese are wild about noodles. They eat them fried; boiled; chilled; tossed with meat, vegetables, and tofu; and warmed in soups and stews.

Mein, as noodles are called in Chinese, have been a part of Chinese cooking for 5,000 years. In fact many historians say that noodles were invented in northern China. Sold

The many flavors of Chinese cooking come together in a meal prepared for a family gathering. Diners use chopsticks to fill their bowls.

A Chinese chef makes noodles the traditional way, pulling, twisting, and stretching them into shape.

fresh or dried, Chinese noodles come in three varieties—wheat, rice, and bean. All three come in varying widths. Because long noodles symbolize long life to the Chinese, noodles are always served long and uncut.

Different noodles are used for different types of cooking. Rice noodles, with their delicate taste, are perfect in soups. Transparent bean noodles have a gummy texture that makes them ideal for cooking with foods that stick to them. Ants climbing trees, a favorite dish, gets it name from the bits of ground pork that cling to these thin noodles.

Wheat noodles, which look and taste like spaghetti,

are a favorite in stir-fried dishes such as chow mein. To make this favorite dish, chefs rapidly fry cooked noodles in hot sesame oil, then toss them with meat, vegetables, and soy sauce. Depending on how long the noodles are fried, they may be soft and tender or crisp and golden. Either way, the noodles, according to Chinese food experts Craig Claiborne and Virginia Lee, "marry well with thousands of flavors and textures."[5] The result is a dish everyone adores.

A steaming hot bowl of noodles appeals to young and old alike.

Chicken and Vegetable Chow Mein

This noodle dish is easy to make. The recipe uses linguini, but spaghetti also works. The noodles should be cooked and cooled before they are fried. The recipe also calls for precooked chicken. Any variety of vegetables can be used, including frozen mixed Chinese vegetables. The vegetables should be cut into small pieces. Shrimp, finely sliced pieces pork, or beef can also be added.

Ingredients:
3 tablespoons vegetable oil
1 teaspoon minced ginger
1 pound cooked chicken tenders, cut into thin strips
1 carrot, peeled and cut into thin strips
1 green onion, cut into thin, round slices
1 green bell pepper, cut into thin strips
1 celery stalk, cut into thin slices

Stir-Fried Delights

Chow mein is just one of many popular stir-fried or chow dishes that the Chinese people love. Stir-frying is an ancient cooking method in which tiny slices of food are cooked quickly over high heat. The Chinese invented it as a way to preserve scarce firewood.

A typical stir-fry dish takes much longer to prepare than to cook. In fact cooking time may be only a minute or two. To stir-fry, the cook chops up ingredients such as meat, seafood, tofu, and vegetables into bite-size morsels. The smaller the pieces, the faster and more

½ cup water chestnuts, drained and cut into thin slices
1 cup bean sprouts
8 ounces cooked linguini
1 tablespoon soy sauce

Instructions:
1. Heat a wok or frying pan over high heat for 45 seconds. Add the oil and heat until it is very hot, about 325°F.
2. Add the ginger, chicken, and all the vegetables. Stir-fry for two minutes.
3. Add the noodles and the sauces. Stir-fry until the noodles separate and are warm.

Serves 4

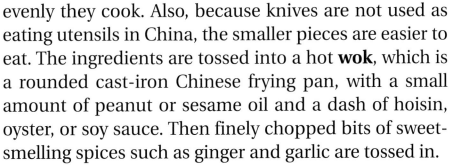

evenly they cook. Also, because knives are not used as eating utensils in China, the smaller pieces are easier to eat. The ingredients are tossed into a hot **wok**, which is a rounded cast-iron Chinese frying pan, with a small amount of peanut or sesame oil and a dash of hoisin, oyster, or soy sauce. Then finely chopped bits of sweet-smelling spices such as ginger and garlic are tossed in.

Now the fun begins. The cook keeps the food in constant motion by tipping and rocking the wok back and forth while stirring the food with a spatula. This allows the food to cook evenly. The rounded shape of the wok makes

Stir-Fry

the process easier, as does the cooking temperature, which must be carefully controlled. If it is too hot, the food burns. If it is not hot enough, the food tastes soggy. When the temperature is just right, stir-fried dishes cook in almost no time and come out crisp and delicious.

Wok Hay

Just about any foods can be stir-fried. Favorite stir-fried dishes include Buddha's delight, a crunchy mix of ten different vegetables. Other favorites mix meat and vegetables. Shredded chicken with bean sprouts is a popular choice.

No matter the ingredients, freshly stir-fried food is always served steaming hot. The steam is known as "wok hay," or "the breath of the wok." For the Chinese, the hotter the dish, the better. They even heat the plates to make sure every bite is piping hot. Young explains: "Wok hay occurs in that special moment when a great chef achieves food that nearly, but not quite, burns the mouth. For the Chinese, if the dish doesn't have the prized taste . . . it isn't an authentic stir-fry."[6]

Sweet and Sour

Many stir-fried dishes blend contrasting flavors. Sweet-and-sour dishes, which originated in eastern China, are a favorite. When carefully balanced, these two opposing tastes form delicious and interesting dishes that tickle the taste buds with a hint of tartness and a lingering whisper of sweetness. To make sweet-and-sour dishes, cooks make a sauce from rice vinegar, sugar, soy sauce, and pineapple juice. The fragrant scent and tangy taste are tantalizing.

The sauce can be combined with all sorts of ingredients. A favorite is sweet-and-sour pork. In this dish, 1-inch (2.5cm) cubes of pork are browned in a wok. Then the sauce and small slices of bell pepper, green onion, bamboo shoots, and ginger are stir-fried and poured over the hot, tender pork. Eaten over rice, the mix of delicious

Names of Chinese Dishes

Many Chinese dishes have interesting and beautiful names. These names, the Chinese say, make ordinary food more appealing. Some foods are named after famous people, like General Tso's chicken, a spicy dish named for a famous Chinese soldier. Other dishes are named after precious gems, animals, or things in nature. For example, stir-fried tofu is known as snowflake bean curd. Stir-fried chicken with broccoli is called jade flower chicken, and stuffed duck is known as eight-jewel duck. Shrimp with bamboo shoots and mushrooms is imaginatively named leaves of wind, frost, and snow. Large pork meatballs are called lion's heads. Although these names tickle the imagination, no matter what they are called, these dishes taste delicious.

Sweet-and-Sour Pork

Sweet-and-sour dishes are not complicated. Chicken, shrimp, beef, or tofu can be used in place of the pork. In some sweet-and-sour pork recipes, the pork is breaded. It is not breaded in this recipe.

Ingredients:

2 tablespoons cooking oil
1 pound pork cut into bite-size cubes
1 cup pineapple chunks, undrained
½ cup water
¼ cup sugar
¼ cup vinegar
1 tablespoon soy sauce
2 tablespoons cornstarch
1 green bell pepper, cut into thin slices
1 green onion, cut into small pieces
1 carrot, cut into small pieces

Instructions:

1. Pour the oil into a pan or wok and heat.
2. Add the pork to the pan. Brown the pork.
3. Drain the pineapple, saving the juice.
4. Combine the pineapple juice, water, sugar, vinegar, soy sauce, and cornstarch in a bowl and mix well.
5. Pour the sauce over the pork. Cover the pan and cook over low heat until the pork is thoroughly cooked.
6. When the pork is done, add the green pepper, carrot, green onion, and pineapple to the pan. Stir-fry for two minutes.
7. Serve with rice.

Serves 4

tastes and textures is unforgettable. It is, according to Yin-Fei Lo, "A dish with balance and complexity."[7]

Fiery Flavors

Hot, spicy dishes are another Chinese favorite. Such dishes use chili peppers and **Szechuan peppercorns** to create fiery dishes with lemony overtones. Not really a pepper, the Szechuan peppercorn is a red berry that comes from the prickly ash tree. It is ground into a powder that has a tangy flavor and a fruity aroma. It is also mixed with cloves, cinnamon, fennel, and anise to create a popular pungent spice known as five-spice powder. The peppercorns contain chemicals that make the tip of the tongue tingle.

By combining chili peppers and ground peppercorns—or five-spice powder—with soy sauce, vinegar, ginger, meat, vegetables, and tofu, cooks create some of China's best-loved dishes. Hot and sour soup is one of everyone's favorites.

A Delicious Cure-All

Hot and sour soup is a made from a rich chicken broth seasoned with ground chili peppers and peppercorns, soy sauce, and rice vinegar. Shredded pork, ginger, bamboo shoots, green onions, and tofu flavor the soup. Cloud ears (fungi that look like flower petals) and lily bulbs (the tiny bulbs that lilies grow from) add beauty and a smoky sweetness to the brew. The final mix tastes lemony, slightly sweet, and incredibly spicy all at the same time.

Women grind bright red chiles into a fine powder that will add fiery flavor to many Chinese dishes.

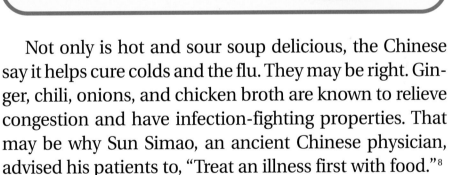

Yin and Yang

The Chinese not only believe that the flavors of food should balance. They say that in order for a person to be healthy, two opposing energy forces in their body—yin and yang—must be in balance, too. Yin is female and cool. Yang is male and hot. Different foods have yin or yang qualities. In order to maintain good health, people must eat a diet that balances yin and yang foods. That is why the Chinese always eat vegetables, which are yin, with meat, which is yang. They also eat bland yin food like rice, with spicy yang foods.

Not only is hot and sour soup delicious, the Chinese say it helps cure colds and the flu. They may be right. Ginger, chili, onions, and chicken broth are known to relieve congestion and have infection-fighting properties. That may be why Sun Simao, an ancient Chinese physician, advised his patients to, "Treat an illness first with food."[8]

Even if hot and sour soup cannot cure illnesses, one thing is for sure. The delicious balance of its many flavors appeals to people all over China. So does the sweet harmony of tastes in stir-fries, sweet-and-sour dishes, and noodles. It is no wonder they are favorites in China.

Chapter 3

Treats That Touch the Heart

The Chinese love to eat. In addition to eating three meals a day, they enjoy mid-morning and mid-afternoon snacks. A steaming pot of tea served with bite-size delicacies known as **dim sum** are a favorite.

Flavorful Dim Sum

The term *dim sum* means "touch the heart." These flavorful treats do just that. Dim sum are bite-size morsels of more than 2,000 different kinds of foods. There are luscious little filled dumplings, paper-thin green onion pancakes, crunchy **spring rolls**, and sweet tofu, to name a few. The variety is almost endless.

The selection is not the only thing that is huge. Most dim sum restaurants serve 1,000 people at a time. Originally

A seemingly endless variety of shapes, sizes, and fillings make up the popular Chinese delicacies known as dim sum.

created as rest stops for ancient silk traders, today they are jammed with Chinese people from every walk of life. They are noisy, busy places where servers, calling out the names of their wares, push carts loaded with dim sum. When diners hear the name of their favorite, they signal the server to their table.

Diners can try as many treats as they want, and variety is the key. Because the portions are small, even people with tiny appetites can sample many dishes. Also, because it is common practice to eat one dish before selecting another, diners are assured that every bite will be fresh and hot. Chinese cooking expert Ellen Leong Blonder explains: "Part of the fun of dim sum is having something hot almost as soon as you sit down, and adding from an endless variety as the meal progresses."[9]

Cloud Swallows

One favorite dim sum is dumplings, which the Chinese call cloud swallows. These plump treats are pastries

Blue Chickens

Many Chinese dishes and dim sum are made with chicken. In China, chicken meat may be white, as it is in North America, or it may be blue black. This interestingly colored meat comes from small Chinese chickens that have dark blue feathers and similarly colored skin underneath. The chickens taste like traditional chicken, but the Chinese say the meat is especially healthy. They often use it to make chicken soup for the sick.

A server in a busy Hong Kong restaurant wheels a cart from table to table, offering diners selections of dim sum.

stuffed with a wide range of ingredients. Favorites include shrimp dumplings stuffed with minced shrimp and chives and pork dumplings made with ground pork, water chestnuts, and mushrooms.

The dough for dumplings is made from wheat flour and water. It is usually thick and chewy. The dough for **wontons**, which are translucent paper-thin dumplings, is made with wheat starch. It is fragile and difficult to work with. For this reason, stores and bakeries throughout China sell ready-made wonton skins.

Whether store-bought or homemade, once the dough is ready, filling and shaping the dumplings take skill. Most dumplings start out as a 3-inch (7.3cm) piece of dough. Cooks spoon the filling onto the dough, carefully fold up the corners, and squeeze the edges to seal the delectable little bundle.

A dab of filling is placed on circles of raw pot sticker dough, and then sealed in by pinching the edges.

A Happy Accident

Most dumplings are steamed in hot water. Some, like wontons, are boiled in chicken broth. The rich flavor of the broth filters through their thin skins and blends deliciously with the filling. In fact, wontons are often served in the broth in a dish aptly named wonton soup.

Dumpling

Boiled and steamed dumplings taste soft and moist.

Dumplings can also be fried until crisp and golden. **Pot stickers**, a favorite fried dumpling, is actually a wonton that is fried in sizzling peanut oil until its bottom sticks to the pan. Then the cook pours hot chicken broth over it. This makes the pot sticker crunchy on the bottom and soft on the top. Chinese legend says that these unique dumplings were invented as a result of a happy accident when a chef accidentally let the emperor's dumplings burn. Rather than admit his mistake, the chef poured hot broth over the dumplings and served them with shredded ginger, green onion, and soy sauce. This practice is still followed today. The emperor loved their taste, just as modern Chinese do. As Young says, they are "Chinese comfort food to warm the soul."[10]

Spring Rolls

Spring rolls are another favorite dim sum. These dainty cylinders are a taste treat. About the size of an adult's

Sweet Soft Tofu

Sweet soft tofu is a popular offering at dim sum restaurants. It is a delicious and easy treat. Tofu is sold in different degrees of firmness. For this dish, soft tofu must be used.

Ingredients:
1 block (1 pound) chilled soft silken tofu
1 cup water
½ cup sugar

Instructions:
1. Drain the tofu. Cut it into four blocks.
2. Put the water and the sugar in a saucepan. Bring the mixture to a boil.
3. Reduce the heat to low and let the mixture cook for about eight minutes, until a syrup forms.
4. Put each tofu block in a small bowl. Pour one-quarter of the syrup over each one.

Serves 4

index finger, they are made with shredded shrimp, pork, bean sprouts, and mushrooms and encased in a crunchy paper-thin wrapper. The wrapper may be made from wheat flour or bean curd sheets. Bean curd wrappers have a nutty flavor. They are softer than wheat but both are scrumptious.

To make spring rolls, cooks stir-fry the filling, spread it thinly across the wrapper, then roll the wrapper up to form a tube shape. The spring roll is fried in sesame oil for about two minutes. Because the cooking time is so short, the oil must be very hot—about 360°F (176.67°C). If it is not this hot, the spring roll does not cook thoroughly and tastes soggy rather than crisp and yummy.

Spring Roll

Originally spring rolls were made in ancient China to celebrate the arrival of spring. They were filled with bean sprouts, which are abundant at that time of year. Today the Chinese eat them all year long. They love to dip them in sweet-and-sour sauce. The combination of the crunchy wrapper, crisp vegetables, savory pork, shrimp, and tangy sauce is incredible. They are, according to Claiborne and Lee, "A dish of pure delight."[11]

Tea

Tea is always served with dim sum. It is far and away the most popular drink in China. The Chinese produce over 200 different varieties. There are green teas, amber-colored oolong teas, black teas, white teas, and scented teas mixed with flower blossoms. They all start out as green plants. What is done to the tea leaves after they are picked determines their color and taste.

Freshly picked tea leaves are spread out in the air to dry. The more oxygen they absorb, the darker they become. This process is known as **oxidation**. Green and white teas do not oxidize. That is why green tea does not change color. Because it has a refreshing clean taste, it is often drunk between courses at large meals. White tea gets its color from the white buds of the tea leaves. It has a mild flavor. Oolong and black tea oxidize. Oolong has a sweet, flowery taste and scent. The Chinese love to sip it with dumplings. Black tea has a robust flavor that often accompanies stir-fried dishes.

The Emperor's Drink

The Chinese have been drinking tea for centuries. Legend has it that the first pot of tea was made in the 3rd century B.C. when a breeze blew a tea leaf into a pot of hot water. Noticing its delicious fragrance, the cook sampled it. The Chinese love of tea was born.

The Chinese have their own way of brewing tea. First they heat water just to the point of boiling and pour it into a ceramic teapot. This heats the pot. The water is then discarded, and tea is added to the pot. Fresh water is poured over the tea leaves. The tea leaves are never added to the water, because the Chinese say this ruins the tea's flavor. They say sugar, cream, and lemon ruin the flavor too. Tea, the Chinese believe, is perfect on its own.

A young woman in Chinese dress performs a traditional tea ritual.

Pot Stickers

This recipe uses commercially made wonton wrappers. They are available in the refrigerated section of many supermarkets. Ground beef or turkey can be substituted for pork.

Ingredients:

¼ pound ground pork
2 green onions, finely chopped
1 egg, beaten
1 teaspoon soy sauce
1 teaspoon sugar
12 wonton wrappers
1½ cups chicken consommé
oil for frying

Instructions:

1. Mix all the ingredients together except the wonton wrappers, consommé, and oil.
2. Put about one-half to one teaspoon of the pork mixture in the center of each wonton wrapper.
3. Moisten the edges of each wrapper with water. Fold the edges up over the filling to form a triangle. Press the edges together to seal.
4. Heat one tablespoon of oil in a wok or frying pan. Put half the pot stickers in the pan and fry without moving them until they are browned on the bottom. This should take about two minutes.
5. Pour in half the consommé, covering the pot stickers. Bring the consommé to a boil and then lower the heat. Cook on a low heat until the liquid is absorbed. This should take about ten minutes. Remove the pot stickers from the pan and repeat the process with the next batch.
6. Serve the pot stickers with soy sauce for dipping.

Makes 12 fat pot stickers

Chinese workers sort tea leaves to be packaged and sold.

The Chinese are so particular about tea that ancient Chinese royalty employed tea masters to supervise its preparation. Whether it is prepared by an expert or in a country kitchen, tea is beloved by everyone in China. Together with crispy spring rolls, crunchy pot stickers, and steaming dumplings, a fragrant cup of tea is a delight. It is no wonder the Chinese cannot resist these wonderful treats.

Festive Foods

China has been called the land of banquets. Since ancient times, the Chinese have marked important occasions with great feasts. It was not uncommon for Chinese royalty to hold banquets in which 365 different dishes—one for each day of the year—were served. The Chinese still love to celebrate with festive foods that make any meal special.

Peking Duck

No Chinese celebration is complete without Peking duck. Made with ducks that have been fed special food to make them extra fat and tender, Peking duck has the reputation of being the most delicious food in China. The way it is prepared is interesting. After the duck is cleaned, air is pumped under its skin with a bicycle pump. This separates the skin from the fat below. As the bird cooks, the fat turns into a rich oil that moistens the meat underneath.

Before the duck is cooked, it is coated with a sweet-and-sour sauce made from rice vinegar and honey. As the duck roasts, the coating caramelizes and turns the duck a coppery red. Before this can happen, the duck is hung to dry for ten hours. This allows the skin to absorb

Costumed waitresses and specially prepared dishes help re-create a traditional royal Chinese banquet from centuries ago.

A chef displays plates of sliced Peking duck, which will be rolled inside steamed pancakes (inset). More ducks hang beside the open fire where they will be roasted.

the sauce better. When it is finally ready for the oven, the duck is filled with broth. This makes it possible for the duck to boil on the inside while roasting on the outside. When the duck is pulled from the oven, the skin is crisp and crackling and the meat is melt-in-your-mouth tender. The taste is amazing.

Rolled in Pancakes

Before it is served, the duck is cut into about 100 slices. These are served with delicate steamed pancakes,

The Kitchen God

The Chinese people love and respect food and cooking. Cooking is so much a part of Chinese life and culture that every Chinese home is guarded by a statue of the Kitchen God. Many Chinese people believe that at the start of the New Year's celebration the Kitchen God reports to the Jade Emperor, the supreme god, about each family. To ensure a good report, Chinese housekeepers thoroughly clean their kitchens and decorate them with flowers before the New Year's celebration begins. They put sweets, water, and soybeans in front of the Kitchen God's statue as a going-away gift. Sugar is placed on the statue's mouth, so the Kitchen God only has sweet things to say about the family. On New Year's Eve, the Kitchen God is supposed to return, hopefully bringing the family best wishes from the Jade Emperor and plans for a happy year to come.

The Kitchen God is thought to bring good fortune to Chinese homes.

green onions, and hoisin sauce. Diners use the green onion like a paint brush. They dip it in the sauce and brush a splash on the pancake. Then they place the green onion on the pancake, add a few slices of duck, fold the pancake over, and enjoy an unforgettable treat. Peking duck has been the centerpiece of Chinese celebrations for 1,500 years. It is, as chef Marc Million says, "One of the greatest dishes of the world and the ultimate duck preparation."[12]

A vendor serves up a bowl of steamy shark's fin soup.

Good Luck Fruit Salad

Fruit is always a part of the New Year's celebration. Its sweet taste promises good luck and happiness in the coming year. The use of ginger in this fruit salad gives it a distinctive Chinese taste. Any combination of canned, fresh, or frozen fruit can be used.

Ingredients:
2 pears, sliced into small chunks
2 tangerines, peeled and sectioned
2 bananas, peeled and sliced into round pieces
1 cup pineapple chunks, juice drained
¼ cup maraschino cherries
½ cup orange juice
1 tablespoon grated fresh ginger

Instructions:
1. Combine all the ingredients in a large bowl and gently mix.
2. Cover the bowl and refrigerate for at least one hour.
3. Serve with hot tea.

Serves 6

Shark's Fin Soup

Shark's fin soup is another Chinese delicacy that is a part of every Chinese banquet. Like Peking duck, it was a favorite of Chinese royalty. Today, because it is so costly, it is considered an honor to be served the soup.

Shark's fin soup is not easy to prepare. Cooks begin with dried fins, which may be whole or cut up and sold in blocks. Whole fins are the most prized and the most expensive. A whole fin from the choicest, most tender species of shark can cost $300 for one pound (0.4kg).

Before a shark fin can be cooked, it must be soaked in water repeatedly to eliminate sand that sticks to it. This can take hours to accomplish. Once this is done, the fin is boiled in water with ginger to get rid of any fishy odors. Next the fin is added to a pot of chicken broth with a small cooked ham, garlic, and green onions. These ingredients give the soup a smoky, savory taste. The mixture cooks for about three hours. The slower it cooks, the richer the flavor. When the shark fin is ready, it will break apart into thin blond strands that have a gelatinous texture. Before the soup is served, the cook removes the ham and saves it for another meal. A mix of cornstarch and water is added to the soup to thicken it. The soup is served in heated bowls and topped with bean sprouts, which the Chinese say look like glistening bits of silver. "No banquet, no feast, of any consequence is considered complete in China unless it includes shark's fin soup," Yin-Fei Lo explains. "This grand classic . . . is especially loved."[13]

The Luckiest Feast of the Year

Eating fine foods at weddings and other important events delights the Chinese, but such events do not always occur on a

A holiday meal is a feast both for the eyes and the stomach.

regular basis. The Chinese New Year, however, does. The Chinese mark the holiday with fifteen days of feasting. The last night of the celebration is the most festive. This is when the Chinese pile the table high with more food than anyone can eat.

Usually eight or nine dishes are served, because both are lucky numbers in China. Among the scrumptious dishes are festive foods that in some way symbolize good

Sweetened Walnuts

Sweetened nuts are a popular New Year's dish. They are often served with fruits and seeds. Pecans can be used in place of walnuts. Be careful not to touch or taste the nuts until they cool.

Ingredients:
1 pound shelled walnuts
6 cups water
1 cup sugar
5 cups peanut or sesame oil

Instructions:
1. Put walnuts in a pot with the water. Bring the water to a boil. Cook for five minutes.
2. Remove the walnuts and drain them.
3. Put the walnuts in a bowl and pour the sugar over them. Stir until the nuts are covered with sugar. The sugar will dissolve from the heat of the walnuts.
4. Pour the oil in a wok or frying pan. Heat over high heat until the oil is very hot. Carefully add the walnuts. Fry for three to five minutes, until the nuts are brown.
5. Cover a platter with wax paper or foil. Remove the nuts from the pan and place on the platter. Use a slotted spoon or spatula so that the oil can drain back into the pot. Leave space between the nuts.
6. Allow the nuts to cool before handling them with your hands. When the nuts have cooled, place them on another platter lined with paper towels. Cover the nuts with another layer of paper towels and gently press down on the top layer of towels to remove any excess oil.
7. Serve with dried and fresh fruit.
Serves 4

luck. A shrimp dish is almost always included. *Har*, the Chinese word for shrimp, is similar to the sound of laughter. Eating it on New Year's Eve is said to bring happiness in the coming year. Stir-fried clams, whose shells resemble Chinese coins, are said to bring wealth. Sweets, which promise sweetness in the new year, and seeds

Kumquats

and nuts, which represent children and fertility, are served throughout the meal. An eight-sided tray laden with tangerines, kumquats, candied peaches, sweetened walnuts, almonds, sliced coconut, and lotus and melon seeds graces almost every table.

Wishes Come True

No matter what else is served, the final and most important dish is always fish. The Chinese word for fish, *yu*, sounds like the Chinese word for *wish*. Eating fish at the end of the New Year's meal is said to ensure that everyone's New Year's wishes come true. Young explains: "It goes with the old Cantonese saying, 'Yu yuen yee sheung,' or, "'May your wishes be fulfilled.'"[14] To bring even more good luck, the fish is served whole with its head and tail still on. This signifies a good start and end to the new year.

The Chinese use only live fish. Trout and carp are popular choices. The fish are kept in tanks and barrels in fish

Steamed fish delicately laden with sauce and platters of cold meats and a variety of seafoods and vegetables make up an exquisite Chinese banquet.

Wasting Food

Because of the many periods of food shortages that the Chinese have faced throughout history, they rarely waste food. Chinese children are scolded if they leave even one grain of rice in their bowls. Parents tell their children that they will get a pimple on their face for every grain of rice they waste. Of course this is not true, but it shows how much the Chinese dislike wasting food. It is not surprising, then, to learn that when cooks prepare Peking duck the parts of the duck that are not used for the main dish, such as the bones, liver, tongue, heart, and kidneys, are served in other accompanying dishes such as soup and pâté. Some cooks make as many as 80 different dishes from the remaining parts.

markets. Cooks select a fish, and the fishmonger kills it while the cook watches. Fish that thrash about trying to stay alive are the most prized. To the Chinese, their struggle for life is a good sign. Eating such a fish is believed to pass on strength and long life to the diner.

Steaming is the most popular way to cook fish. First, however, the fish is **scored**. This means that the cook makes diagonal cuts in the fish's skin. This helps the fish cook more evenly. Many Chinese cooks tuck slices of ginger and green onions into the pockets the cuts form. These give the fish a tantalizing scent and flavor. Before the fish is steamed, salt is rubbed over its skin. Then it is placed in a bamboo steamer basket that sits in a wok filled with boiling water or broth over high heat. The basket is covered so that moist heat from the boiling liquid can circulate through the fish. When the fish is ready, the cook removes the cover carefully, because the burst of steam that escapes when the cover is removed is boiling hot.

Hot sesame oil and either soy or oyster sauce is poured over the cooked fish. It is served on a bed of rice. The fish tastes so moist and tender that it melts in the mouth. Clairborne and Lee say: "There is no food more delicate than genuinely fresh fish steamed properly, Chinese fashion. It has a purity that is perfectly complemented by whatever sauce it is served with."[15]

It is no wonder that the Chinese celebrate with steamed fish just one of the many festive foods that make holidays and special occasions noteworthy and fun.

Metric conversions

Mass (weight)

1 ounce (oz.)	= 28.0 grams (g)
8 ounces	= 227.0 grams
1 pound (lb.) or 16 ounces	= 0.45 kilograms (kg)
2.2 pounds	= 1.0 kilogram

Liquid Volume

1 teaspoon (tsp.)	= 5.0 milliliters (ml)
1 tablespoon (tbsp.)	= 15.0 milliliters
1 fluid ounce (oz.)	= 30.0 milliliters
1 cup (c.)	= 240 milliliters
1 pint (pt.)	= 480 milliliters
1 quart (qt.)	= 0.95 liters (l)
1 gallon (gal.)	= 3.80 liters

Pan Sizes

8-inch cake pan	= 20 x 4-centimeter cake pan
9-inch cake pan	= 23 x 3.5-centimeter cake pan
11 x 7-inch baking pan	= 28 x 18-centimeter baking pan
13 x 9-inch baking pan	= 32.5 x 23-centimeter baking pan
9 x 5-inch loaf pan	= 23 x 13-centimeter loaf pan
2-quart casserole	= 2-liter casserole

Length

1/4 inch (in.)	= 0.6 centimeters (cm)
1/2 inch	= 1.25 centimeters
1 inch	= 2.5 centimeters

Temperature

212° F	= 100° C (boiling point of water)
225° F	= 110° C
250° F	= 120° C
275° F	= 135° C
300° F	= 150° C
325° F	= 160° C
350° F	= 180° C
375° F	= 190° C
400° F	= 200° C

Notes

Chapter 1: A Common Thread

1. Eileen Yin-Fei Lo, *The Chinese Kitchen.* New York: William Morrow, 1999, p. 177.

2. Grace Young, *The Wisdom of the Chinese Kitchen.* New York: Simon and Schuster, 1999, p. 6.

3. Yin-Fei Lo, *The Chinese Kitchen*, p. 3.

Chapter 2: A Harmony of Flavors

4. Quoted in Lee Su Jan, *The Fine Art of Chinese Cooking.* New York: Gramercy, 1962, p. 19.

5. Craig Claiborne and Virginia Lee, *The Chinese Cookbook.* New York: HarperCollins, 1972, p. 357.

6. Young, *The Wisdom of the Chinese Kitchen*, p. 21.

7. Yin-Fei Lo, *The Chinese Kitchen*, p. 414.

8. Quoted in Rhonda Parkinson, About Chinese Cuisine, "Food as Medicine," http://chinesefood.about.com/library/weekly/aa092200a.htm.

Chapter 3: Treats That Touch the Heart

9. Ellen Leong Blonder, *Dim Sum.* New York: Clarkson Potter, 2002, p. 12.

10. Young, *The Wisdom of the Chinese Kitchen*, p. 16.

11. Claiborne and Lee, *The Chinese Cookbook*, p. 366.

Chapter 4: Festive Foods

12. Marc Million, Quay Press, "Notes from a Devon Kitchen," www.quaypress.com/winefood/devonkitchen/duck.html.

13. Yin-Fei Lo, *The Chinese Kitchen,* p. 147.

14. Young, *The Wisdom of the Chinese Kitchen,* p. 105.

15. Claiborne and Lee, *The Chinese Cookbook,* p. 207.

dim sum: Bite-size morsels of various Chinese foods. Many are stuffed pastries.

dumplings: Small balls of cooked dough.

fan: The Chinese word for rice.

fermented: A food that has gone sour as a result of a chemical change.

mein: The Chinese word for noodles.

oxidation: A chemical reaction that occurs as a result of exposure to oxygen.

pot stickers: Dumplings that are fried on the bottom and steamed on top.

scored: To have cut small slits into meat or fish before cooking.

soy sauce: A salty sauce made from fermented soybeans.

spring rolls: Fried cylinders filled with pork, shrimp, and vegetables.

steamed: Cooked by moist heat.

stir-fry: A cooking method in which food is cooked rapidly over high heat.

Szechuan peppercorns: A spicy fruit used to make hot and spicy dishes.

tofu: A food made from soybean curd.

wok: A rounded pan used for stir-frying.

wontons: Thin Chinese dumplings.

For Further Exploration

Books

Theresa M. Beatty, *Foods and Recipes of China.* New York: Power Kids, 1999. This children's cookbook has recipes from different regions of China.

Matthew Locricchio, *The Cooking of China.* New York: Benchmark, 2002. This is a kid's Chinese cookbook.

Holly Schroeder, *China ABCs.* Minneapolis: Picture Window, 2004. This is an alphabet book filled with facts about China.

Nina Simonds, Leslie Swartz, and the Children's Museum of Boston, *Moonbeams, Dumplings, and Dragon Boats: A Treasury of Chinese Holiday Tales, Activities, and Recipes.* New York: Gulliver. This book talks about Chinese holidays and includes fun activities, legends, and recipes.

Stuart Thompson, *Chinese Festivals.* Chicago: Raintree, 2001. This book contains fun and interesting information about three festivals and how they are celebrated.

Web Sites

About Chinese Cuisine (http://chinesefood.about.com). Offers dozens of recipes, information, and stories about Chinese food.

A to Z Kid's Stuff (www.atozkidsstuff.com/china.html). Facts, activities, and stories about ancient and modern China with a lot of interesting and fun links.

Foodnetwork.com (http://www.foodnetwork.com/food/ 1f_kids/article/0,1904,FOOD_16382_3468033,00. html). This page for kids talks about the food of China and contains links to five recipes.

Think Quest (www.thinkquest.org/library/search.html). This Web site offers dozens of links to information about Chinese history, art, inventions, culture, travel, and food.

Time for Kids (www.timeforkids.com/TFK/hh/go places/main/0,20344,536982,00.html). Designed for kids, this Web site lets visitors take a virtual tour of the Great Wall, learn about Chinese history and culture, send e-postcards, and hear Chinese spoken.

Index

Picture credits

Cover Image: Lonely Planet Images/Getty Images
AFP/Getty Images, 41, 44, 50
Brand X Pictures/Getty Images, 24
© Dave Bartuff/CORBIS, 37
© Dean Conger/CORBIS, 42
Eyewire, 46
FoodPix/Getty Images, 10, 13 (lower), 27, 32, 34, 47
Iconica/Getty Images, 49
Lonely Planet Images, 12, 14, 31
Lonely Planet Images/Getty Images, 26
© Nik Wheeler/CORBIS, 9
© PhotoCuisine/CORBIS, 22, 33
Photodisc Blue/Getty Images, 35
Photodisc Green/Getty Images, 15, 29, 45
PhotoDisc, 8, 13 (upper), 48
© Royalty-Free/CORBIS, 42 (inset)
© SETBOUN/CORBIS, 18
Stockbyte Platinum/Getty Images, 21
Stone/Getty Images, 19
Suzanne Santillan, 5
The Bridgeman Art Library, 43
The Image Bank/Getty Images, 6, 17, 39

About the Author

Barbara Sheen has been an author and educator for more than 30 years. Her writing has been published in the United States and Europe. She lives in New Mexico with her family. In her spare time, she likes to swim, garden, walk, and bike. Of course, she loves to cook!